FRENCH LEAVES

ENTRÉE DE VILLAGE

COROT

From the picture in the Louvre

FRENCH LEAVES

BY

E. V. LUCAS

ILLUSTRATED CHIEFLY BY

ARTISTS OF THE BARBIZON SCHOOL

PHILADELPHIA

J. B. LIPPINCOTT COMPANY

1931

PRINTED IN GREAT BRITAIN

INTRODUCTION

THESE 'leaves' bring together a number of stray descriptions of French towns, French works of art, French inns and French journeys, with a eulogy of a great Frenchman here and there, all written from time to time in the past few years, with no connecting link but France itself and the author's interest in France, his curiosity there, and his enthusiasm.

By way of illustration I have chosen nine paintings from the Thomy-Thierret collection in the Louvre, not because they bear directly upon the text of the book, but because they are the kind of French picture that I like best and because they show France at its tenderest. To these I have added a little Corot, presented to the Louvre by MM. Christian and Maurice Robert in 1926, and never before reproduced, a Monet from the Tate, and a recent landscape by M. Josué Gaboriaud.

If any French words in these pages are wrongly spelt it is because they have escaped the vigilant eye of my friend Mr. de V. Payen-Payne, who very kindly read the proofs.

E. V. L.

October, 1930

v

CONTENTS

LIST OF ILLUSTRATIONS

All the illustrations, with the exception of 'Entrée de Village' by Gaboriaud and 'Les Peupliers' by Monet, are from photographs of pictures in the Louvre by Les Archives Photographiques d'Art et d'Histoire, Paris.

FRENCH LEAVES

THE CLUBLESS CLUB

IF you would become a member of 'The Clubless
Club' of France—Le Club sans Club—you
must buy a book entitled *Les Auberges de France*,
published and edited by M. Paul Poulgy at 42,
Rue de Trévise, Paris. It costs fifteen francs.

Les Auberges de France, the organ of Le Club
sans Club, covers the whole of France, making Paris
the starting-point for mileage: equal attention thus
being given to the needs of the visitor to, say,
St. Cloud and St. Germain, Hendaye and Lille,
Quimper and Cap d'Antibes. To those eating-
places that have special character a note of description or laudation, or both, is appended, and where
at the end of this note you find the letters CSC.
(Club sans Club) you may be more than ever sure
of content. The mere possession of the book con-
stitutes membership, and to display its cover as
you enter is (or should be) to receive preferential
treatment.

1   1

The Committee, in their preface, ask that when you have been disappointed by a restaurant you will let them know; when you have been pleased you will thank the proprietor and drop the Committee a line. Finally, they say, if you have found the Club sans Club useful, make yourself its trumpeter: 'Speak well of it to others. If they won't listen to you, break off all relations. See that your companion (if you have one) does the same. If she refuses, divorce her. A true gastronome ought never to be crossed.'

The arrangement of facts is very clear. Eleven Paris gates are taken in turn, and the main roads leading from those gates are followed, as far as three hundred kilometres, with all the best houses of call noted in turn. We begin with the Porte Maillot, the first restaurant on the route being at Rueil, eight kilometres away, where three places are named—Giquel, Le Merle Franc, and the Restaurant Fournaise—and the last at Cherbourg, three hundred and twenty-five kilometres, where you are advised to go to the Hôtel du Casino, to the Hôtel du Grand Balcon, or to the Hôtel de l'Etoile. The last gate is La Porte de la Chapelle (or La Porte de Clignancourt), where the first stopping-place is Saint-Denis (Restaurant Chotard), eight kilometres, and the last Calais, two hundred and sixty-six kilometres, where the Restaurant de la Taverne des Trois Suisses gets the palm.

The restaurants are classified under various descriptions: P.B., P.M.B., M.B., H.B., cuisine excellente, cuisine soignée, cuisine réservée, cuisine suffisante, cuisine X, and so forth. P.B. means Petite Bourgeoisie, or for clients who come by train. P.M.B. means Petite et Moyenne Bourgeoisie, rather better quality, for clients who come in cars as well as by trains. M.B. means Moyenne Bourgeoisie, or for clients who come only by car. H.B. means Haute Bourgeoisie, for clients who want the best. Cuisine excellente means a table perfect from every point of view, but without too much ceremony. Cuisine soignée means a table that conforms with the best old French traditions, but has a simple and even familiar service, where the chef is a conscious artist. Cuisine réservée means that not enough is known by the editor, or that his collaborators differ. Cuisine suffisante explains itself. Cuisine X means that nothing is known at all. Grand confort means electric light, running water, and communicating bath-rooms. Confort means that there is a bath-room somewhere. Petit confort means less even than that, with the assurance that the rooms are 'coquettes et propres'. Armed with this book the motorist should find a trip in France far more pleasant than if he started out without any guidance at all.

The description of such places as I know gives
me confidence in the work.   There is, for example,
the Hôtel de l'Yvette, at Saint-Remy-lès-Chevreuse,
thirty-six kilometres from Paris by the Porte de
Saint-Cloud.   The editor says that it has a justified
renown, and I agree with him.   He says that the
kitchen is admirably controlled by Madame Yvon,
the hostess, and I agree with him.   He says that
the service is 'peu rapide', and I agree with him.
The spécialités are a terrine de canard, poisson à
la manière d'Yvon, and légumes au jardin.   All are
good.   The garden slopes down to a little river and
is most excellently kept by a gardener who never
ceases to smoke a pipe from which the stem has
almost disappeared.   I can add to the spécialités
de la maison an apple-tart cooked while you
wait.

The range of auberges begins with Suresnes,
seven kilometres from Paris, and finishes with
Strasburg, four hundred and forty-seven kilometres,
the arrangement of the routes being according to the
gates from which one leaves the city.   Between
these two extremes are nearly four hundred pages
of gustatory information and glee, including an
amusing chapter on the Livre d'Or, which consists
of extracts from various visitors' books all over
France, in which famous people have written
epigrams.   M. Maeterlinck, for instance, at the

restaurant Chez Raoul, at Chantemerle, between Mantes and Vernon, wrote :

> Tu cherches le bonheur passant!
> Ecoute un peu:
> C'est là-bas 'chez Raoul'
> Le nid de l'oiseau bleu.

M. Maeterlinck's Raoul, by the way, who used to be at the Café Napolitain in Paris, is so popular that he has to stand in the doorway on Sundays turning people away. 'I'm sorry, but we're full up,' he says; 'but down there, nearer the river, you'll find an excellent and cheaper house, run by an old circus clown.' The book, of course, is not only one of inns and dishes, but also of hosts and hostesses. On every page one sees them vigilant and welcoming at the door, suave among the tables or busy in the kitchens. Many have left Paris restaurants to cater for the road: the famous Jean, for example, of La Tour de Claire at Vernon, used to be at the Cochon d'Or in the Avenue Jean-Jaurès. Some are more than restaurateurs, like M. Wolff at the Hostellerie du Lion d'Or at Pacy-sur-Eure, who is a banker and financier as well, but does not let that interfere with his care for his guests. Some are strictly 'regional', like M. Gaston Meunier at the Auberge Saint-Pierre at Dampierre, opposite the château, whose cooking comes from the Jura; others, like M. Potier of the Hostellerie de la

Garenne at Rambouillet, have a kitchen whose secrets are well guarded. M. Cuquemelle, of the Claridge Hotel at Reims, is the most smiling of all: 'to see him directing the service, hovering over the tables, talking with the guests, is to gain the impression that he works not for a living but for sheer pleasure.' That is the way!

Les Auberges de France is indeed a very amusing book, with far more French character tucked away in it than in any novel or sociological work I have read for a very long while. The scouts of the CSC. (for, of course, one man could not cover so much ground or eat so many meals) have been chosen with discretion, and all bring gusto to their reports, not unmixed with humour, so that even those readers who do not want to eat may be amused. Thus, at Auxerre, at the Restaurant de la Tour d'Orbandelle, where M. Huré, fils, works so hard for the comfort of his guests, we are told that Alice Cocea, the actress, left the testimony, 'Mon petit ventre reconnaissant'; while at Chenonceaux, should your companion, on hearing that the superb château there was given to Diane de Poitiers for her beautiful eyes, reproach you with avarice, you are advised to lead her at once to the Hôtel du Laboureur and show yourself as gallant and generous as you can be allowed to be for eighteen francs, less wine. At the Restaurant de l'Huisne at Le Mans there

LE CHATEAU DE ROSNY

COROT

From the picture in the Louvre

is a collection of eighteen hundred liqueurs from seventeen different countries. 'What a beautiful excursion if one could taste them all!'

Incidentally, one learns from this book that Napoleon, in addition to other trifling feats, was the inventor of the cocktail. Although the most frugal of eaters and drinkers, allowing only eight minutes to lunch and twelve to dinner, he was assisted, it seems, in his 'miracles of endurance and activity' by 'a mixture of different alcoholic spirits, of which he himself controlled the dosage'. So testify Bourienne, Fouché and the valet Constant Wainj, who served him from 1801 till 1814; while Marchand, who succeeded Wainj and accompanied his master to St. Helena, left among his papers the recipe of the ex-Emperor's favourite pick-me-up, which has just been put on the French market. It seems to be what is called a 'Rose', but I cannot say what the ingredients are, and a 'Rose' seems to be differently mixed wherever it is ordered. Still, a 'Rose' for me in future. Who would not cock his tail in such company?

With this magnetic book in your hand you will be enabled to see, no matter by which gate you leave Paris, how quickly the true country begins and how good it is. Perhaps to say 'no matter which gate' is a little misleading, for some of the suburbs last longer than others; but the country will sud-

denly come, and it will be true country, washing
right up to the confines of the little old towns, many
of which are a full century behind the Parisian
clocks. One of the most surprising things is the
number of great estates ringed by their own walls:
the château, the park and the wood; but few of
the mansions are to-day unshuttered. Where the
families live I cannot say, but not in the old ancestral
homes. When these places are rightly maintained,
you may be fairly sure that they have passed into
the hands of some rich merchant or manufacturer.

The little towns, however, give no sign of decay;
they go on in their accustomed way, very much as
they did in the days of the Second Empire, their
façades no less white, their roofs no less steep, their
housewives no less voluble, their pavé no less uneven.
There may be a new assemblage of jerry-built
abris in the neighbourhood of the station, which,
although the abodes of whole families, are little
bigger than the huts in our English allotments;
but that is all that is modern. The motor-cars
tearing through the narrow streets have done no
more than tear through: they have left no mark.
Between car and car the ancient peace reasserts
itself.

RABUTIN

RANGING Normandy, one goes to Caudebec for its old houses, of which the Maladerie is chief, its old church, its admirable inn, the Hôtel de la Marine, and for the spectacle from its windows of the big ships gliding past from Le Havre to Rouen or from Rouen to Le Havre and the open sea: strange objects amid these green fields. One goes to Pont-Audemer on the river Risle for its old façades, for its church, and most of all for an ancient tumble-down tannery, all gables and points and timber and grey tiles, which has been turned into one of the best inns in France, the Auberge du Vieux Puits, where, in addition to things to eat and drink, you will find enough old domestic articles to stock a dozen antiquity shops. Tanning was, of course, the great industry of Normandy—William the Conqueror himself was a tanner's grandson—and you will find tanneries new and old everywhere, but none so comely as the Vieux Puits.

Turning to the account of the excellent inn of the Vieux Puits given by *Les Auberges de France*, I find that it is suggested that when you arrive, as

a stranger, it might be as well if M. Constant
Pasquier, the proprietor, in order to punish you for
not having been there before, refuses to serve you
at all! M. Henri Kistemaekers has written in its
Visitors' Book that to know old Normandy, to appre-
ciate Flaubert, and to call oneself a gourmet, it is
necessary to stay at this inn; while another guest,
more epigrammatic, writes: 'When one speaks of
ordinary wells (Puits) one thinks of Truth, but
when one thinks of these Old Wells (the Vieux
Puits) one talks gastronomy.' High praises; but
I think the Vieux Puits deserves them, not less on
account of its structural charm, its comfort and odd
curiosities, than because it keeps live trout from the
Risle in a pool in the middle of the courtyard, with
a contiguous net to pull them forth and bear them
to the kitchen. And the hors d'œuvres used to be
of a wider variety than most inns offer, comprising,
for Pont-Audemer (as the name implies) is near the
sea, small crabs of peculiar succulence and the
freshest of shrimps. But I am in danger of being
thought materialistic. Let me, therefore, again draw
your notice to Pont-Audemer's architectural beauties,
its church, its post-office (an old eighteenth-century
mansion, with fourteenth-century blotting-paper),
and the ruins of Notre-Dame-du-Pré.

One goes to Le Pin-aux-Haras to see the horses,
but one must also eat, and with this agreeable end

in view one naturally consults our reference book. *Les Auberges de France* remarks of the Tourne-Bride, the inn there, that 'if you chance not to know of this hostellerie you will be wise to conceal that fact, or you will be taken for a convict who has escaped after forty years in gaol. However that may be, if you haven't a clear conscience, be very careful about going there, because the boss is the Mayor. . . . His excellent food is served in a very picturesque setting. Take the Calvados 1878, and you will be rejuvenated for months.'

Whether the house is living up to this reputation I leave to the reader to discover; but even were I able to flit about Normandy as I should love to do—with the apple blossom making the valley of the Risle enchanted ground—it would be rather to see if Rabutin was still in his stall than to consume old Calvados brandy. For Rabutin is of all horses my favourite: a white stallion of gigantic proportions, smaller only than an elephant, with a benign head, great shining eyes destitute of the ordinary bright alarm, and the most comforting curves and rotundities, as of the South Downs in the afternoon. His quivering upper lip is proof enough that the horse, the rhinoceros and the tapir are of the same family. In my memory Rabutin holds first place among the prize stallions of Le Pin-aux-Haras, which is the great breeding station of Normandy, that country

of cart-horses, where tractors still are rarely seen
and motor-cars seldom belong to farmers.

The activities of Le Pin-aux-Haras proceed
around a château of the seventeenth century, which
would be worth visiting for itself alone, with its
terrace overlooking an undulating park; but with
the added allurement of these noble animals of the
finest blood, the place is attractive indeed.   There
are some famous racing sires here too, but the great,
kindly, lumbering cart-horses please me most, and I
like to see them thus honoured.   Race-horses are
always in the limelight, perhaps too much so; it is
good now and then to see the gentle, massive
Dobbins there too, and chief of them the darling
colossal Rabutin, who surely is still the pride of
the shire section, for he could not be allowed to
die.   Did I tell you of his benign head, his friendly,
unaffrighted eyes, his nuzzling nose, his snowy
mane?   And his nervous little whinnying to draw
attention away from the others, did I tell you of that?
Well, let me do so now. 'My beautiful, my
beautiful!'

ON THE YONNE

I SUPPOSE that somewhere, in a dryasdust book of reference, I could find the number of rivers, great and small, in France; but, except for the pleasure of reading their names, I do not really want to know how many there are, because the information would carry with it the melancholy thought that to explore or even see them all is now an impossibility to me. No time, no time. But what a great number there must be is obvious to anyone moving about that country: from the wide rivers with locks and leisurely, talkative lock-keepers to the narrow rivulets, not, however, too narrow to have pretty names and to be gravely fished by men in blue linen jackets. It is a long time since the *Liber Fluviorum, or River Scenery of France*, with engravings after one J. M. W. Turner, was published—nearly eighty years, in fact—and someone with plenty of leisure and enthusiasm should do the work again, and do it better than its author, Leitch Ritchie, even if a better illustrator was not to be obtained. A grander certainly could not be; but to Turner the rivers of France meant not serene

and shining streams winding between soft meadows
fringed with poplars and sedges, but water highways
notable less for their quiet reaches and curves than
for the circumstance that from their banks rose
cathedrals, gabled roofs, and embattled fortresses;
because just as Dr. Johnson, in Goldsmith's phrase,
made minnows talk like whales, so did Turner
elevate the humblest villages to the rank of cities of
romance. For the true illustration of any book on
the rivers of France the gentle Corot and the sincere
Daubigny would be as important as the English
magician. Well, none of these three exist any more,
but thank whatever powers may be that new artists
are born every day and some of them very good.
I could, without consulting a catalogue, name at least
six with whom a voyage of discovery among the
rivers of France would be an enterprise of singular
delight.

One of my favourite French rivers is the Yonne,
which rises somewhere in Burgundy, I believe, and
turns into the Seine at Montereau. I came upon
it first with startling suddenness, approaching Sens
from Nemours, where I had left behind me the
Loing, another placid stream. Three or four miles
short of Sens the road turns and abruptly descends,
and there before you is the Yonne valley, with the
ancient cathedral city, once ecclesiastically more
important than Paris, and between you and it a

chain of modern factories. Even in the venerable heart of the place the present jostles the past, for the principal street is the high road from Paris to Lyon, and the courtyards of the two inns are on this road, and the cathedral square is on this road, and on this road there is the unceasing traffic of motor-cars urged on their wild career by members of a nation wholly insensitive to discordant sounds.

Under these conditions of unrest it is not easy to reconstruct Sens when it was a stronghold of the Church and a harbour of refuge to Thomas à Becket, Archbishop of Canterbury, after one of that 'turbulent priest's' worst quarrels with Henry II. Becket had taken shelter with the Cistercians at Pontigny, but when Henry threatened to expel all Cistercians from England if the Abbot of Pontigny did not withdraw his hospitality, the Archbishop moved on to Sens, and you will see in the beautiful white cathedral an uncouth piece of sculpture brought from his house. Becket was then merely an English primate on bad terms with his King and not too well placed with Rome, since in those stormy times there were rival Popes; but after he had been assassinated and canonized, Sens became very proud of him and set up a pictorial window and named a chapel in his honour.

But Sens was an accident in my progress, just as its river was, for I was impelled to this particular

journey by the wish to see Auxerre, the motive
power being the story of Denys l'Auxerrois in Pater's
Imaginary Portraits. But as, however, the more I saw
of the Yonne the more I fell under its fascination, the
result was that to the river I gave most of the time
intended for Auxerre, and to Auxerre far too little.
Instead of going right on to Auxerre I found an
inn on the Yonne's very banks and stayed the night
there, and all through the night was conscious of
the song of the first nightingale of that year coming
across the water. I forget the name of the village
where this inn was situated, but it was not far from
one of France's myriad Villeneuves—Villeneuve-
sur-Yonne—compressed within walls, with a moat
all round and two Gothic gateways, one at the north
and one at the south—just as the Three Musketeers
and d'Artagnan would have known it. In England
there would long since have been a by-pass, but the
French do not trouble about such amenities, nor
have they any unemployed to make them, so I
suppose that for many years to come the thousands
of cars on the Lyon-Paris road will continue to
rush through this narrow pavé street, past the shops
and shopkeepers, the church and the town hall,
without offending any native ear or depriving the
inhabitants of one moment's sleep.

How different was my retired hostelry, with no
sound but an occasional barge by day and the

LE MATIN

TROYON

From the picture in the Louvre

nightingale by day too and when day was done!
How does Pater, in his deliberate way, adding cell
to ceil, like a bee, describe it? 'The Yonne,' he
says, 'bending gracefully, link after link, through a
never-ending rustle of poplar trees, beneath lowly
vine-clad hills, with relics of delicate woodland here
and there, sometimes close at hand, sometimes leaving an interval of broad meadow, has all the light-
some characteristics of French riverside scenery on
a smaller scale than usual, and might pass for the
child's fancy of a river, like the rivers of the old
miniature painters, blue and full to a fair green
margin.' Not unlike the course of the Yonne itself,
this cautious, prehensile, lambent prose!

If you wish to continue to believe in Pater's
story of the Greek youth reincarnated in the French
provincial town, his early joyfulness and his gradual
decline to melancholy and death among Christian
antipathies, it is unwise to pay Auxerre a personal
visit. Better to leave it all vague and wistful, as in
the book. For Auxerre bustles, and even in the
cathedral it is difficult to capture the mediæval
spirit. Nor could I find any such antiquity shop
as that in which the weaver of this fantasy chanced
upon the fragment of stained glass that set him
upon his task. I liked the narrow streets, the
massive west front of the cathedral, with its sombre
graven figures, the bishop's palace, the benedictory

2

figure of St. Germain, the gateway with the clock, but I could find no trace of the pagan efflorescence which Denys brought to this country of vineyards and vine-dressers. Such are the divisions of poetry and prose; such is the unwisdom of analysing the rainbow's warp and texture. But if you want a good bottle of Chablis, Auxerre is the place.

CITIES OF THE DEAD

FRANÇOIS DE LA CHAISE, who gives his name to the great Paris cemetery, was born in 1624, of aristocratic descent, the grand-nephew of Père Coton, confessor of Henri IV. Becoming a Jesuit, he was for many years a popular lecturer on philosophy at the University of Lyon. Whether he had set before himself as an ideal the emulation of his grand-uncle, I cannot say; but at the age of fifty he was appointed confessor of Louis XIV, and thenceforth for many years was an influence behind the throne. His first considerable achievement was the severance of the monarch from Madame de Montespan, the ascendancy of Madame de Maintenon being, to his mind, far less undesirable and indeed a blessing; and it was he who, when Louis married that remarkable lady, performed the ceremony. As a domestic diplomatist Père La Chaise, whose personal conduct seems to have been of the highest, was more successful than in larger politics, for France never recovered from the renewed dissension between Catholics and Protestants following the revocation of the Edict of Nantes, in 1685, in which the King's confessor was a prime mover. Indeed, with that revocation most of her troubles both at home and abroad began.

Père La Chaise died in 1709, at his home on the hillside that is now covered by the graves of dead Parisians, and it is that circumstance which gives the cemetery its name. The municipality of Paris acquired the property from the Jesuits about a century later, chiefly for the needs of the north-east district, in which it is situated, but ever since then illustrious Frenchmen and Frenchwomen have been buried there as though it were a national resting-place.

Walking through this wonderful but very tiring city of the dead, one is continually being stopped by honoured and thrilling names. There is no grave here quite so moving, to me, as that of Heine, in the cemetery of Montmartre; but in the range between the tomb of Abélard and Héloïse, at the foot of the mountain, and of Oscar Wilde, at the summit, what a world of once ardent energy lies still!

I mention these two tombs in particular, not merely because they are so widely separated, but because it is these that, according to an attendant, most English visitors ask for. Indeed, it is to the tomb of Abélard and Héloïse that nearly all sight-seers, the French also, first make their way—to the right on entering the Porte Principale. These

disastrous lovers are grouped in our minds with
Romeo and Juliet and other couples of romance,
but they were real enough in their day, which was
the twelfth century, and they are peculiarly of old
Paris, Abélard having (like Père La Chaise himself)
taught philosophy and theology in his school on the
hill of St. Geneviève, and later having been a recluse
in the Abbey of Cluny, where the museum now is;
while Héloïse was the daughter of one of the canons
of Nôtre Dame. Their tragic story need not be
told again; it is enough to say that, after their part-
ing, Héloïse became a nun and Abélard a monk,
and late in life, when Héloïse was head of Abélard's
religious order at Paraclete, near Nogent-sur-Seine,
the two used again to meet. It was the composition
of Abélard's *Historia Calamitatum* that drew from
Héloïse the 'Letters' in which her side of the piteous
liaison found its expression. Abélard died in
1142, at the priory of St. Marcel, near Châlon-sur-
Saone, and was buried there; but Héloïse contrived
that his remains should be brought to her at Paraclete, and when she died, in 1164, she was buried
beside them. After other removals, they were
reinterred at Père-la-Chaise in 1817, beneath a
Gothic canopy built from fragments of the ruins of
Paraclete by Alexandre Lenoir, the painter. The
two lovers, in stone effigy, may be seen side by side.

What other tombs can I recall? I saw Alfred

de Musset's, with its willow tree just bursting into leaf under the hot spring sun; I saw the last resting-place of the beloved Corot, and, close by, of Henri Daumier, to whom Corot gave a house and was a friend when most that unworldly genius needed one. I saw the graves of Rachel, of Sarah Bernhardt, of Talma. Rossini and Auber, Cherubini and Chopin all have tombs here, although Rossini's remains were transported to Florence not long ago. I saw the family vault and chapel of the Hertfords, where Sir Richard Wallace, of the Wallace Collection, lies. I saw the tombs of Molière and La Fontaine, of Charles Nodier and Alphonse Daudet, of David, who painted the famous portrait of Madame Récamier, and of Géricault, who painted race-horses, of Balzac, and of Béranger.

If you would stand by the graves of other favourite authors and artists and musicians you must go to the cemetery of Montmartre, just off the Boulevard Clichy. Alexander the Greatest is not here, but here is his son, Dumas fils. Heine, as I have said, lies here, brought from his 'mattress grave', as he called his bed, at No. 3 in the Avenue Matignon, in 1856. Among the composers at Montmartre are Ambroise Thomas and Offenbach, Délibes and Hector Berlioz. Among the painters are Greuze and Delaroche, Ary Scheffer and Troyon; among the authors, the brothers de Goncourt, Théophile Gautier,

Henri Murger (who invented the Latin Quarter, if not Montmartre too), Meilhac, the cynical dramatist, and Renan, who would humanize Christ.   Zola was buried here, but only his monument remains; he was reinterred in the Panthéon, where Victor Hugo already lay.   At the Panthéon you will find also the graves of Rousseau and Voltaire.

Voltaire's statue, a rather too pompous out size, is by Houdon.   If you would see the grave of Houdon himself, that most entrancing of modern sculptors, you must go to the Cemetery of Mont-parnasse, in the Boulevard Edgar-Quinet, which dates from 1824.   Here, again, the names that have become household words are on every side: Sainte-Beuve lies here, and François Coppée, Théodore de Banville and Guy de Maupassant, Leconte de Lisle and Baudelaire, with the Spirit of Evil to guard him.   Among the artists are Jules Breton and Fantin Latour, Charles Garnier, the architect of the Opera, and the sculptors Rude and Bartholdi. Among the musicians are Saint-Saëns and César Franck.   The etcher Méryon lies here, but his grave is desolate and its description illegible.

LES COURSES

I. ST. CLOUD

AS I was standing, one afternoon, in the paddock on the St. Cloud racecourse, watching a number of horses, each looking to my untrained eye like a winner, yet all but one of them —and that wholly unsuspected—certain to falsify my hopes, I was tapped on the shoulder, and, looking round, recognized an English acquaintance, whose sole greeting was the question, 'Who was St. Cloud?'

Who, indeed?

I had been to St. Cloud races many times; to the fête of St. Cloud often; and to the Pavillon Bleu for refreshment as seldom as possible, for it is far too dear; but never before had I concerned myself with the identity of the holy man who gave the suburb his name. Still, I was not to be beaten. 'Just now,' I replied (more or less), 'I am not in a position to enlighten you. The pressure of horse-flesh is too insistent, and I still have money to lose. But give me time to return to a more studious environment and you shall know. Meanwhile, have you any tip for the next race?'

Unfortunately he had.

Once again in touch with my old allies, the books of reference, I learned that St. Cloud was a grandson of Clovis, King of the Salian Franks from 481 to 511. Clovis, who was a pagan, married Clotilda, a Burgundian princess and a Christian. During his war with the Alemanni he promised that if Clotilda's God would give him the victory he would be baptized into his wife's faith and add his influence to it. Success being his, he was as good as his word, and such was the delight of Heaven that a special phial of holy oil was borne to the ceremony by a celestial dove. From this victory Clovis passed on to others, until he became King of all France, with Paris his capital, and it was he who framed the Salic law. Such was the grandfather of St. Cloud.

The saint's father was Clodomir, Clovis's second son, King of Orleans, and on his father's death the youth was brought up with his two brothers, by his grandmother Clotilda. His name then was Clodoald. On being rescued from his wicked uncle Clotaire, King of Soissons, who desired his death, he cut off his hair and devoted himself to a life of piety in a retreat which stood somewhere on the site of the town that now bears his name: Cloud being the diminutive of Clodoald. As it also has the same sound as 'clou', a nail, the saint was chosen by nailsmiths as their patron. 'Hence, since horses wear shoes, there is a certain appropriateness, my dear sir' (I should have said to my friend, had not all my erudition been an affair of the escalier), 'in the place where we are now standing and doing ourselves no good, being called St. Cloud.'

Our own St. Leger, by the way, is even more remote from the Sport of Kings than was St. Cloud. He also was of French courtly traditions, his father having been in service under Clotaire II in the seventh century. He became a priest, an abbot, and finally Bishop of Autun, and on that town being besieged gave himself up in order to save it from destruction. The foe put out his eyes and later he was assassinated. His halo was the reward for such a death and in honour of his charitable deeds.

II. AN INNOCENT ABROAD

An amusing article could be written around the foibles and eccentricities of dusky and other potentates and notabilities sojourning in England, just as in the East (if they had that kind of curiosity) an amusing article could be written around the oddities of illustrious G.T.s from the Occident. For there is always something comic about the foreigner.

LES PÉNICHES

DAUBIGNY

From the picture in the Louvre

Upon such an essay I do not at the moment propose to embark, but—passing from St. Cloud to Longchamp—I here offer what might be an instalment of it, although in the end the emphasis will be found to be laid rather upon one of the potentate's Western entertainers than upon himself. I garnered the material from that most admirable newspaper, written by French gentlemen for French gentlemen, the *Figaro*, in an article by M. Gheusi, the theme of which is the humours of the late good King Sisovath, ruler of Cambodia, when he was the guest of Paris twenty and more years ago, during the Presidency of the massive and benign M. Fallières.

Sisovath liked Paris, and Paris liked Sisovath. In the sympathetic leading-strings of the Colonial Secretary the Indo-Chinese monarch was taken everywhere and saw everything, and thus it happened that in due course, by way of the opera, of the cinema (of which it was his first glimpse, and at which he was terrified by a charge of cavalry coming straight at him from the screen), and of the studio of M. Rodin, whose sculpture gave him great satisfaction, he reached Longchamp.

The occasion was a Sunday afternoon, and the King was installed in the President's own box. The President himself was absent, but before the day he had minutely instructed his deputy as to his line of conduct. 'I count on you', said he, 'for the success of the occasion. The welcome must be worthy of the King, to whom you will explain the mechanism of our races and instruct him in the breeding and training of our bloodstock; in fact, tell him everything you know about horses.'

The Colonial Secretary listened, but said nothing. He did not dare to admit that when it came to horses and racing his mind was a blank; he had never even risked a franc at petits chevaux. 'And, of course,' the President added, 'you will explain the pari-mutuel, for the King will inevitably want to have something on.'

The Colonial Secretary, once at liberty, lost no time. . . .

The first race was one of those dreary foregone conclusions, when the favourite wins 'in an armchair' and everyone is found to have backed it. They are the despair of English punters in France, because for every ten francs you get only, say, twelve-fifty, which does not include the stake. The King, however, although his winnings were small, was delighted. In the second race he won again, and again was pleased, more particularly as many members of his suite had picked losers. The next race, however, was one of those memorable dramas, fortunately also not too rare on French courses, when an outsider upsets all expectations and is returned at an enormous figure. The record, I believe, is held by a steeplechaser at Auteuil, named York II, who was so dark a horse that he actually reached the five thousands. There was no such price on the occasion which I am describing, but the odds were gratifyingly heavy—let us say 33 to 1.

'I suppose', said the King, looking anxiously at his host, 'I can hardly have won this time.'

'As it chances,' replied the Colonial Secretary, 'I was lucky in finding the winner,' and he handed the King a bunch of tickets.

Sisovath was at first dumb with surprise; then his features shone with an effulgence of rapture, and, seizing the hands of his entertainer, he gazed upon him with a mixture of the admiration and awe that are reserved only for those with supernatural gifts.

In the fourth race, which was again an ordinary event, the King won again; and then came the last, which was to have been another certainty, but which ended in a bouleversement of form even more astonishing than in the third, the King receiving tickets from the sorcerer (as he now believed the official to be) bearing odds of 50 to 1.

When Sisovath, on the eve of returning to his own country, took leave of the President, he asked a favour. 'Will you', he said, 'allow me to borrow for a while the services of the gentleman who has been showing me round? He is the most marvellous judge of horses imaginable, and we want someone of that kind to advise in improving our studs.' To this M. Fallières made a tactful non-committal reply, and, when the King had left, sent for the Colonial Secretary to acquaint him with the request and its implied compliment.

'It is absurd,' said that official. 'I know less than nothing of horses. But in order to meet your wishes that the King should not lose, I was careful to take tickets for every one of the runners, and, when the time came, to hand to his Majesty only those for the winner.'

'Not a word to the King, I implore you,' said M. Fallières, as his not inconsiderable frame shook with merriment, 'and we will find a pretext to keep you here. He must never know the truth. It is inexpedient that our honoured and distinguished guests from overseas should hold any but the highest opinions of the ability and acumen of the personnel of the Colonial Office.'

Some years later, says M. Gheusi—with whose narrative I have, by the way, taken many liberties, although I hope retaining its spirit—King Sisovath was recounting his Longchamp adventure to a guest from Paris.

'And Monsieur Blank,' he asked, mentioning the wizard, 'is he still at his old post?'

The Parisian replied in the negative; the gentleman had quitted the administrative career for private pursuits.

'A pity,' said the King; 'a most capable and delightful man; and what a judge of horseflesh!'

STATUES OF HEROES

PHOTOGRAPHS in the newspapers of two sculptured representations of Lord Haig on horseback—one, a statuette, for the Mess of the 17th Lancers, and one, full-size, for Montreuil-sur-Mer—sent my thoughts to the fine Foch memorial at Mont-Cassel, and I saw again the quiet, alert figure of the French commander, on his steed, both in imperishable bronze, as he looks out from this astonishing eminence across the fields of battle. He is 'a horseman in the sky' indeed, for Mont-Cassel rises from the plain, as abruptly almost as a pyramid, to a height of more than five hundred feet, and the statue has been placed in a little garden on the very summit, only a few yards from the great soldier's headquarters, where, with the eyes of life, he must so often have scrutinized the same landscape—but then how different in its tragic turmoil.

Those who cannot travel to Cassel can see what this statue is like by looking at its replica near Victoria Station, but they will require much imaginative vision to realize its dominating position on that French summit.

Mont-Cassel's broad Place, with its fine ancient façades and the few tributary streets, lies well below, the last stages of the climb to the memorial being almost painfully steep; but when you are there you can rest, while an elaborate scheme of orientation on the parapet of the escarpment tells you exactly what towns and cities are to be seen; or rather the direction in which they lie, for most are out of sight. That it is a comprehensive survey you will agree when I say that the extreme westerly city is Dublin. Why Dublin? Tipperary would be more appropriate. The choice has been very capriciously made, for although Manchester and Liverpool, Birmingham and Leeds, have each their arrow, London is not mentioned, nor is Dover. The places which, under favourable conditions, are visible, have two feathers to their shaft instead of one: such as Ypres and Cambrai and other historic centres of the fray. No monument to a general could be more thrillingly set than this, or as thrillingly set, for Mont-Cassel is unique.

For the benefit of any readers who may be contemplating a motor tour in the French and Belgian war zone, I may say that Montreuil-sur-Mer, where the French statue of Lord Haig is erected, is unique too, but in another way. It is unique in not being on the sea at all. Centuries ago it may have been, but to-day the Channel is nine miles distant, and the

only water is a narrow stream called the Canche.
As an inland fortified town, with a citadel and ramparts and some ancient ecclesiastical buildings,
Montreuil is, however, charming, as thousands of
artists have discovered. The British headquarters
were at the Château de Beaurepaire.

The late catastrophe was by no means Cassel's
initiation in warfare. As long ago as the Roman
conquest of Gaul it was fortified and known as
Castellum Menopiorum, while there were battles
here in 1071, when Robert, Count of Flanders,
overcame Arnulf; in 1328, when Philip of Valois
defeated the Flemish, and in 1677, when Philip,
Duke of Orleans, vanquished William of Orange.
In the year following, Cassel became French.
Having read these facts on the other and much
older monument on the top of this remarkable hill,
it is well to descend to the Place again for lunch,
and this you can consume very comfortably in a
sunny room belonging to the Hôtel du Sauvage,
whose windows give on to a western panorama
hardly less vast than that of the north and east from
the Foch parapet. Photographs of the Maréchal,
who used to eat here, are on the walls, and it is
doubtful if there is better butter in the world.

Two other pieces of sculpture I should like to
mention while I am writing about the department
of the Pas de Calais, both of which may be of

LES CHAUMIÈRES

COROT

From the picture in the Louvre

interest to the English motorist. Should Calais be his headquarters, he will, of course, see Rodin's group of the Burghers of that town, which stands in the Place d'Armes in front of the Musée. These were the six citizens, led by Eustache de St. Pierre, whose story Froissart tells so movingly. The surrender of the fortress (on August 5, 1347) was to be made, Edward III stipulated, by these men in their shirts, with halters round their necks. Having handed him the key, they were to be executed. But Queen Philippa, who was with the King, interceded for them on her knees 'for the love of Our Lady's Son', and the King granted her request. Rodin's group, of which we have a replica in the Victoria Tower Gardens in London, does not include Edward III or Philippa. I mention it here for the reason that, in its position in the Place d'Armes in Calais, the Burghers are raised only a few inches above the level of the ground, whereas at Westminster they are on a high pedestal. Which position is right? Clearly both cannot be. It would be interesting to know what the sculptor's views were, and also what the sculptors of to-day think about it.

My last piece of statuary is the monument to Latham, the English airman, isolated on a bleak turf down, on the sea road between Calais and Sangatte. He stands in a negligent, easy posture on a mass of stone looking out over the Channel, much as the bronze Foch at Cassel looks over the plain of France and Belgium. The aviator is dressed in an ordinary lounge suit, with a cap and a scarf with loose ends. In his left hand is a cigarette in a holder; his right is in his coat pocket. For its perfect naturalness and graceful poise I associate this figure with Donatello's David, in the Bargello, with Alfred Gilbert's St. George at Windsor, and with Thornycroft's Gordon in Trafalgar Square.

OLD FRENCH TRAVEL

IT is difficult to keep pace with those zealous, loyal and imaginative Frenchmen who devote their energy to the celebration of their illustrious compatriots. Considering how little—superficially—the individuals of France seem to be concerned with others, how concentrated they are on their own purposes, it is remarkable that so much time and thought should be given to the glorification of their dead. But no people, I suppose, are so jealous of the fame of their great men. This statement may be proved not only by noting the names of French streets and the profusion of statues, but by reading the newspaper reports of this and that new unveiling, conferences of the admirers of famous dramatists, poets and painters, or the opening of museums in their praise. Beneath the surface of the Paris life which the ordinary English visitor sees, how much of what might be called spiritual patriotism is in progress! Whatever ethical seriousness the Frenchman is supposed to lack—and when alone he probably lacks none—he more than makes up for in devotion to his country's finest flowers.

The museum which has provoked these reflections is dedicated not to any one creative career but to the history of road travel; yet the assembling called for no less care and labour. The next time you visit Compiègne you will find in the palace, in one of the wings, this Musée de la Voiture et du Tourisme, and I think you will agree that it is worth examination. But you must not expect too much. The whole history of road travel would need more room—the Grand Palais itself, where the annual motor show is held, could not do justice to it—even if French exhibits alone were accepted. As a matter of fact, to leave a Paris show-room containing the latest marvels of automobilism—both of the chassis and the body—and spend an hour on a trip to Compiègne and back (it is only seventy-five kilometres away) would be a lesson in evolution, for the very earliest cars are on view there—high, draughty, rickety affairs, more obsolete than the ichthyosaurus.

Those earliest cars! I remember so well the day when, after a traction engine's flag-staff had been broken in two in Northumberland Avenue by a pioneer of motoring, a procession of automobiles solemnly and hopefully started on their way to Brighton, where there was to be a lunch in honour of the new vehicle and the new liberty. I don't know how many set forth, but only a few got there, one of which, seen in the distance by a Sussex friend of mine as it passed on the skyline somewhere near Clayton, led to a happy conceit. It was his first sight of one, and 'I felt', he said, 'as though I had suddenly been deprived of the power of seeing horses'. Well, the kind of car that bewildered him all those years ago—was it 1895?—you will find at Compiègne; but no others, for the Musée de la Voiture et du Tourisme stops at the first. It has the first bicycles too, preceded by boneshakers and velocipedes; but no others.

To me most interesting were the posting carriages, for the more I move about the world in cars and trains the more I am astonished at the curiosity, courage and endurance of our travelling ancestors. The surface of roads, off the main routes—and in France even on the main routes, with their perplexing alternation of good tarmac, bad tarmac, potholed tarmac, gravel and pavé—is still often bad; but think what it must have been everywhere a hundred years ago. You can get an idea of it to-day from the approach to the Palace of Versailles, which no one has ever troubled to make smooth. Remembering the jolts that are there one's lot, it is almost an incredible thought that in 1830 the Comte de Damas should have ridden from Paris to Jerusalem in the carriage which is one of the principal Compiègne treasures. I have no knowledge as to the size of the party, but, with any approach to comfort, there is room inside only for two. Outside there is a back seat for three, one of whom had to work the brake. Three padlocked boxes for the sugar-loaf hats of the postilions are a permanent fixture. The luggage was disposed under this back seat, under the box seat, and in flat cases fitting exactly over the roof. Inside, opposite the seat, are racks and pockets and a shelf. There are four windows, rather more easily lowered and raised than those of the modern London cab, and candles for night. The carriage lights consist of three big lamps in front; none at the back. There is a skid for the front wheels.

In this lumbering and congested conveyance the Comte de Damas, exactly a century ago, had the hardihood to travel from Paris to Jerusalem. He must have had a very strong reason for going there —stronger than any Zionist could muster. When I recall the distaste for foreign adventure that is one of the Frenchman's most emphatic characteristics, I marvel afresh; but most do I wonder how he got back, for nothing is said of the return journey. Perhaps he laid down his bones there with a sigh of relief that he was to ride in this coach no more.

Among the other carriages is a coupé de voyage which leads to reflections that go beyond mere discomfort. This is the very vehicle in which Napo-

LE FENDEUR DE BOIS

MILLET

From the picture in the Louvre

leon, after escaping from Elba, posted from Grenoble to Auxerre. It is all in black, the seat is very low and the floor-space is reduced by the necessity of accommodating the folding steps on each side. What were the thoughts of the Emperor as the weary miles dragged on? Dreams of new conquest and power. Fears and hopes, hopes and fears. A tragic carriage indeed.

In addition to these elaborate conveyances you will find simpler things, such as the forerunner of the hansom, dated 1760, which, on account of its limited accommodation, was called the 'Disobliging', and a diligence of the last century which ran between Cap Corps and Cheval à Gap, wherever they may be, with a sheep-bell to forewarn its approach and a wooden chest with powerful locks for valuables. There are also such accessories as old harness, old liveries. A suit of one of Napoleon's own postilions may be seen, with the whitest of white breeches and Imperial badges. Where there are no originals there are models by the historical painter Maurice Leloir, and old prints by the hundred; so you see that an ideal of thoroughness has been followed even if expansiveness is impossible.

But what I thought a sign of true inspiration is the room upstairs fitted like a posting inn of the eighteenth century, with figures of host and hostess as large as life, and a pair of guests, not impossibly elopers. This has been arranged with much thoughtfulness and the result is surely very like the real thing. The models are good, whether of human beings or hams and sausages, while the genuine details scattered about, such as saddlebags and bottles, chairs, crockery and fire-irons, and luggage, add to verisimilitude. All that is lacking is the cheerful noise of the place: the landlord's deep tones as he commends his cellar; the landlady's assurances of only a 'little minute' longer; the crackling of the logs; and the lovers' murmurs of satisfaction in being at last at their ease. Even more perhaps does one miss the kitchen's scents and savours.

SAINT TROPEZ AND ITS ADMIRAL

IN the search for summer heat, as everyone now knows, the South of France has been rediscovered. To visit it in the winter has long been a mechanical act; although by me to be avoided, for its winter radiance is not a cordial, beneficent outpouring, but fitful and treacherous, followed at twilight by a perilous fall in temperature. But to visit the South of France in summer, anywhere between Hyères and its islands and Ventimille on the Franco-Italian frontier, is to be assured of tropical skies and a sea of a pleasing tepidity. Having rejoiced under torrid rays in many parts of the earth, I can give it as my considered opinion that the South of France can, even though this be a delusion, convey the sensation of greater heat than the Equator itself.

Far from the coolest of the French watering-places which are so steadily gaining popularity is St. Tropez, in the department of Var, an ancient seaport of mixed ancestry which lies on the south bank of the Gulf of St. Tropez, between Toulon and St. Raphael, on a coast fragrant with myrtle

and pines. Each year the number of house-agents'
notice-boards, offering desirable lots, increases, particularly on each side of St. Maxime, from St.
Aygulf on the east to Beauvallon on the west,
where a delicious vin rosé is grown; but St. Tropez
itself is comparatively safe, for—not a mushroom
settlement for sun-beetles, like these others—
every inch that can be built on has been built on
for many, many years.

Although, however, the town is fixed, about it
are villas springing up, not a few occupied by
English residents whose instinct for finding delect-
able refuges to which Somerset House officials cannot penetrate is becoming infallible. These villas
are extending to Ramatuelle, a hill-top citadel,
from whose ramparts the Mediterranean glitters
so gaily. It was from Ramatuelle that the inevitable invading Saracens were repulsed in the dark
ages by a very odd weapon indeed, and probably
far more efficacious than boiling oil, molten lead,
or any missile: none other than swarms of bees.
'I'll set my bee at you!'—that was a terrible
threat.

Like Marseilles, St. Tropez probably had a
Phœnician origin. Its present style came in the
second century, after the holy and steadfast Tor-
petius, an early Christian, had been put to death
there, Tropez being the Gallicization of this name.

Then, as part of the fixed routine of Provençal towns, came destruction by the Saracens, not once but twice, and, in the tenth century, rebuilding under Guillaume the First, Count of Provence. More vicissitudes were, however, to follow, for in the struggle between the Duke of Anjou and Charles de Duras in the fifteenth century, St. Tropez was again demolished, and, although restored, had become to the natives so unattractive a seaside residence that strong repopulating methods were necessary. An emissary was therefore despatched to the crowded city of Genoa, which, I suppose, even then had a fecund look, to put before the eyes of some specially-selected fruitful Genoese the delights and advantages of the French seaport. The ambassador was so plausible that, on St. Valentine's Day, 1471, twenty-one married couples of Genoa, with their young families, disembarked at St. Tropez to make their homes there. Hence the high Italian façades of certain of the houses on the quay; hence the blend of Italian and French blood which the sociologist may discern to-day in many of the inhabitants.

The more visible population of St. Tropez when I was there was, however, composed of artists, with and without the final 'e', from the two Parisian mountains—that of Parnassus and that of the Martyr—and invaders from Mid-Europe. The

mountaineers were the more noticeable, bringing
with them, I was told, their incorrigible tendency
to turn night into day. Certainly those around
me who, in the principal café on the quay,
were preparing their weary systems for lunch,
gave no sign of having come to the seaside for
any of its usual benefits, which here are aug-
mented by spécialités of the town in the form of
nougat and gaudy but attractive coats for the
fair, made at St. Tropez, and, I believe, at St.
Tropez only, out of the peasants' coloured hand-
kerchiefs. Indeed they may be said to have
brought Paris with them and to be intending to
keep it.

But the glory of St. Tropez is its local hero,
the sturdy admiral, who is to be seen in bronze,
on the quay, facing his old element, with chain-
shot at his top-booted feet and a megaphone
(is it?) in his hand, and far too many heavy clothes
on. But a fine, aggressive figure, none the less.
This admiral was the great Suffren—or, in full,
Pierre André de Suffren Saint Tropez (1729–88),
bailli of the Order of Malta—son of the Marquis
de Saint Tropez who was, in his day, the overlord
of this domain, and whose massive house still
stands, close to the Genoese quarter. If he had
had a Suffren, Napoleon is reported to have said,
he would have made short work of Nelson and the

English navy. The bailli's early years gave him every opportunity of studying naval tactics, even though he was infrequently on the winning side. When only eighteen he was taken prisoner by Hawke. In 1756 he was a lieutenant in the Orphée, in the battle of Minorca, when the defeat of the English fleet brought about Byng's ruin and execution. But not till 1781, when in command of a squadron, was Suffren able to assert his dogged individuality. Then, says David Hannay, in commenting upon the action at Porto Praya in 1781, when Suffren routed Commodore Johnstone, he proved to the English that 'in him they had to deal with an admiral of quite a different type from the Frenchmen they had been accustomed to as yet'.

The solid pugnacity of the great bronze head tells you that here was a determined foe. All through 1782 and 1783, off the coasts of India and Ceylon, he was harassing Hastings and Hughes, and nothing, it is said, but the lack of support given him by certain of his captains, who were not used to such vigour and address, kept him from sweeping our ships from those seas. He died, in harness, at the age of 59, some records say of apoplexy, and some that he was killed in a duel to which he had been provoked by the Prince de Mirepoix, who asked him to perform an act of nepotism discreditable to an admiral of France and a bailli of the Order of Malta, and detrimental to the best interests of the Navy. On refusing, he was challenged, and fell.

A FRENCH SMOKER

ONE does not, naturally, look to a Frenchman for a eulogy of tobacco. Of wine, of cooking, of love—yes; but not the weed. For the French as a people use tobacco in too thoughtless a manner: almost wholly in cigarettes, or in shocking cigars supplied to them by an insensitive and jealous Government and sold in shops presided over by soldiers' widows whose methods are purely mechanical. Pipes are infrequent, and, such as they are, are viewed by English smokers with suspicion if not positive dislike—with a few exceptions, of course, chief of which, in my own eyes, is that sacred specimen preserved in a glass case in the Moreau-Nelaton collection in the Pavillon Marsan in the Rue de Rivoli: the pipe which reposed between the lips of Corot. As a pipe it is inadequate, inferior; as the solace of that best of Frenchmen and painters it is to be worshipped. It is true that in Paris to-day there are shops where English pipes (made, as it happens, of French briar) are to be bought, and I have no doubt that, although these shops exist chiefly for visitors, it is

the thing for young French bloods to endeavour
to smoke them; but for the most part the French,
like all Latins, prefer the cigarette; and if they
smoke a Havana cigar it is only after a meal, and
as part of that meal.)

I was therefore the more surprised to receive
the other day a little memoir on the herb of herbs,
entitled *Eloge du Tabac*, by M. Maurice des Ombiaux,
in which the place of the divine leaf in history,
in literature, and in our affections is very agreeably
stated. And always from the French angle; there
is no mention of our famous English smokers:
Maeterlinck but not Tennyson, Baudelaire but not
Barrie. Many contemporary poets are called upon
to sing the praises of their Lady Nicotine, including
M. Tristan Derème, who seems to have kept his
versatile Muse busy, for he begins some verses
with the confession:—

> J'ai tour à tour chanté l'ombre, des roses transitoires,
> L'azur, les escargots, l'amour, la pipe et les étoiles.

M. des Ombiaux quotes the beginning of another
poem, by Sacha Guitry, which tells us that Corot
is not alone among the pleinairistes as a great
smoker.

> Honneur de la Peinture et du Tabac français,
> O grand Claude Monet, je veux t'offrir ce livre.
> Toi qui n'arrête pas de fumer et de peindre,
> Fumant pour ton plaisir et peignant pour le nôtre !

ENTRÉE DE VILLAGE

JOSUÉ GABORIAUD

From the picture in the possession of the Author

Old Harpignies, I expect, smoked too.   Assuredly
he enjoyed his liquor.

And now for M. des Ombiaux himself, on the
faith that is in him.   After naming all kinds of
pipe, including the clay so dear to Charles Keene,
and the meerschaum, now, in England, practically
obsolete (the reds of summer and the dying tints of
autumn, in the colouring bowl, move him to ecstasy),
he says: 'For our own part, the best of pipes we
consider to be that made from an old briar-root;
one which can easily be cleaned and may be relied
on to draw well.   With such a one it would seem
to be that the flavour of the smoke is less a matter
of material concern than with others, for you taste
the tobacco in all its purity, this being also accompanied, almost imperceptibly, by another aroma,
that of the briar-wood, an adorable alliance with a
plant such as is bound to enchant you.   Yes, the
briar-pipe does, indeed, seem the best and most
perfect as a medium for thorough enjoyment,
where the smoker of tobacco is concerned.   The
pipe of the true smoker, once gripped between
his canine teeth, does not budge; indeed, it
would seem to form an integral part of his
jaw.'—For a Frenchman that surely is very hand-
some!

Here is an historical passage, also roughly
turned into English: 'The pipe has conquered

the world: sailors and soldiers have been its propagators. There can be no doubt that without tobacco military service would be more irksome than it is.

'When summoned to Versailles by Louis XIV the heroic Jean Bart lit his pipe in the ante-chamber of the great King!

'The conquerors of Austerlitz and of Jena returned to Paris with their pipes between their teeth. The habits acquired in the field made their way into the most sumptuous of hotels—and from that time onward public resorts fell, conquests to tobacco.

'The Restoration, which had retained all the prejudices of the past, was hostile to the weed: an attempt was made to put it down, condemning it as associated with bad habits, and, at Court, it met with nothing but disfavour. Yet was it too late, for public opinion had definitely adopted the custom, and notable examples were put forward in extenuation thereof: Ney, bravest of the brave, had lit a cigar when setting out to the place of his execution, and the sergeants of La Rochelle awaited death with their pipes between their lips.'

M. des Ombiaux is interested in tobacco, not only nationally, but locally. I knew that there were briars and tobacco plants in the South, round and about Montpellier, but I had not thought of France as really producing its leaf. I had thought that the horrible tobacco which one buys in France when one has finished one's own comes from Morocco or Algiers. But M. des Ombiaux advocates an intensive patriotism in those who smoke it. Thus: 'French soil, so varied and so rich, offers many gradations of precious flavour to the smoker. Why, then, should the productions of the different provinces be reduced to one uniform type? The scale composed of French tobaccos is without doubt as rich and varied as is that of French wines. Why, then, neglect such a source of profit, so great a satisfaction to our senses?'

And so we come to the seductive but mysterious Obourg and semois. 'I, who am of the Sambre-et-Meuse, believe I prefer the Obourg and semois, not because I am of the same soil, but because these tobaccos have a fullness of flavour and an aroma which proclaim them to be chefs-d'œuvre of their kind. At a meet, after having refreshed oneself with a greengage, a fine plum, or some calville of the fields, a pipe of Obourg can double the charm of the hour. And then, along the tracks made in the woods for the placing of traps, whither the succulent hares wend their way in order to get themselves caught, how delicately the aroma of the semois blends with the scent of the damp leaves!'

Both Obourg and semois are unknown to my own particular Mr. Godall; but the next time I go to France I must try both. M. des Ombiaux makes them as alluring as the Arcadia Mixture.

BOURGES

FOR the last three or four years one of the greatest travellers of our times—his mileage throughout most of the countries of the globe tops the million—has asked me, periodically, if I have yet seen Bourges cathedral; for although his principal interest is metallurgy, he has an eye also for architecture. And hitherto I have always had to say no. But when he next arrives, suddenly, from whatever corner of the earth he may at this moment be investigating, I shall be able to say yes. Why I have been so long in visiting Bourges is one of those mysteries of life which are always with us, the answer being that the clock had not struck; for I have wanted to go there, planned to go there, and more than once started to go there. We all have our Bourges, our inaccessible Meccas; but now, through having found it, this one of mine is lost.

Having seen Bourges—the town and the cathedral—I am in the position to be pityingly surprised at those who have not been so sage as I, and eloquently urgent that they should go there. 'You haven't seen Bourges!' I can exclaim, in the accepted manner. 'Extraordinary! Nothing could be simpler than the journey from Paris; just over two hundred kilometres on Route Nationale 20, tarmac from start to finish, and Orleans exactly half-way. Two hundred kilometres is one hundred and twenty-five miles—an easy two-day trip. You can spend the first afternoon at Orleans, and see the Joan of Arc museum, and follow her story in coloured glass in the great church; you can sleep at Bourges; and on the way back look in at Chartres to compare notes, and be dining in Paris as usual that evening. Bourges! Why, of course, you must see Bourges! How anyone can miss it is beyond understanding.'

The cathedral of Bourges stands where it should, and where cathedrals stand too seldom: on the highest plateau of the town. It spreads over the summit of the hill with enough room for a view of all sides and the proper appreciation of its towers, its buttresses, and the myriad circular windows and decorative spaces that form a great part of its exterior charm, most impressive of which is that of the portail meridionale. Over all is the long silvery-slated roof, with a coping of lead; and it is interesting to note how gently and sympathetically the rigid level line of this roof lies like a hand on the restless turmoil of masonry below it and soothes it into harmony and quietude. Within, the inner of the

two aisles, lofty and glorious, reminded me of
Amiens, but there is not the same coldness. A
little very rich old glass remains, but the other
glass fills one again with dismay at the want of
taste that so often marks those who control ecclesiastical windows. The frames are exquisite in design
and workmanship, but the hues that fill them are
deplorable.

Falling into the hands of a sacristan enthusiast
who was under the dominion of the word 'Merveil-
leux', I was shown the Romanesque crypt merged
with the terrifically solid Roman stonework built
when Bourges was Avaricum. The outer temperature on this August day was near a hundred Fahren-
heit: the cathedral was far from cool; but the crypt
struck such a chill that (God forgive me!) I was
emboldened by the presence of these pagan founda-
tions to replace my hat. Two of those articles of
headgear, by the way, are allotted places of honour
in this noble fane and stimulate the sacristan to an
emotional excitement almost as intense as that which
he experiences, or affects to experience, before the
statuary group of the Deposition in the crypt
itself: the hats, suspended high in the central aisle,
being those of two cardinals who are buried here.
Among other of the lions are the massive recumbent
figure, in white marble, of Duc Jean de Berry, one
of the builders of the cathedral, with a broken nose

and the autographs of thousands of sightseers
scratched or pencilled upon him, and the kneeling
figures of the same genial old autocrat and his first
wife, for ever with their marble hands clasped in
prayer, before a little chapel in the apse.   Three
other devotees in marble you will find in another
chapel—the Chancelier de l'Aubespine, his wife,
and their son, the Marquis de Chateauneuf: so
lifelike that they might have been overcome by the
dust of a volcano and fixed for all time as symbols
of piety.

The cathedral, however, is not all; there remains
Bourges; and Bourges strikes me as a very distinguished town of which its inhabitants are justly
proud.   I refer to the old residential parts, often
dating from the Middle Ages, where the houses are
all different and all architecturally interesting, where
there is no dirt and no squalor, but comeliness and
care, and where little seems to be of the present
day.   (Alas, since my visit many have been destroyed
by fire.)   The old régime is suggested at every
turn.   Natural, one feels, that there should be a
whole building devoted to the office of that impeni-
tent Royalist sheet *L'Action Française!*   Below and
around the altitude on which this old Bourges is
built spread factories and arsenals and market
gardens, for modern Bourges works as hard as any
French industrial town—and that is saying not a

LA ROUTE D'ARRAS

COROT

From the picture in the Louvre

little. But the Bourges that remains so graciously
in the memory is the Bourges of the named and
narrow streets, of gables, towers, and statues, of
fountains and public gardens, all capped by the
grey glory of the cathedral.

One of the most famous of these Bourges edifices
is the palace of Jacques Coeur, a romantic figure of
the fifteenth century, who began by being a simple
merchant; went on to develop trade with the East,
like another Marco Polo; and made so much money
out of silks and spices that in 1448 he became Minister
of Finance to Charles VII, lending him money for
his wars and executing diplomatic errands. It was
then that he built this palace, now the Law Courts,
which is notable both for its general distinction and
for two of the most charming carved chimney-pieces
I have ever seen. Put not your trust in princes!
Jacques, like so many of the too prosperous, was
soon in disgrace, and his last years were spent in
the service of Popes Nicolas V and Calixtus III,
fighting against the Turks. But his statue and his
palace, with its two chimney-pieces, and his chapel
with its motto indefinitely repeated, 'A vaillans
cœurs riens impossible', keep sweet his fame in his
native town.

PAINTER, BANKER AND KING

HAVING long been an admirer of the painter Théodule Ribot, I was delighted to find myself in the little Normandy town of Breteuil-sur-Iton, because it was at a neighbouring village, St. Nicolas d'Attez, that he was born, in 1823, and a bust of him has been erected at the beginning of the long and broad grass alley bordered by trees leading to the château: a bust with the typical head of a clever Frenchman, with an overlapping velvet cap, as of a Montparnasse artist on the stage, falling on one side. I was glad to find Ribot thus honoured, because of all the great painters of his period—he flourished for the thirty-five years preceding his death in 1891—he is, I should say, the least known, or so my own inquiries would indicate. Few of the people normally interested in art of whom I have asked the question, 'Don't you think Ribot a great painter?' have had any knowledge of his work at all. He did not paint much, nor did he seek popularity. His favourite subjects are old peasant or bourgeoise women bearing on their wrinkled countenances the

traces of the hard lessons that life can teach.   They
are not vindictive, not sordid: merely experienced,
and, though perhaps disillusioned, not bitter but
philosophic about it all.   'C'est la vie.'   These
heads, which represent the artist's most character-
istic bent, remind one now of Rembrandt, now of
Ribera, but are in no sense imitations of these
masters: essential Ribot.   The prevailing tone is a
rich brown.   Ribot took his subjects also from those
who are at the other and gayer end of life, boys and
girls, and he was fond of introducing domestic
utensils and articles of food, all done in the grand
rather than the Dutch manner; but it is his old
women that I see when I close my eyes.   Yet how
seldom one finds these pictures!   There are six at
the Luxembourg, chiefly representing his scriptural
work; there are some of his old people in Edinburgh.
The Wallace Collection knows him not, nor does
our National Gallery, but at the Tate there are
two or three examples on loan from the Burrell
Collection.

Ribot is not the only eminent man that Breteuil-
sur-Iton honours in sculpture.   In the middle of its
place, in a central enclosure, is the bust of a very
different type: Jacques Laffitte, the banker, who is
here by virtue of tenancy of the château and not
local birth.   He was, as a matter of fact, born at
Bayonne and was one of the ten children of a

carpenter. That was in 1767. Thirty-three years
later he became a partner in the banking firm of
Perregaux, which he had entered as a clerk (although
not, so far as I know, performing the other customary
and symmetrical feat and marrying his employer's
daughter), and ultimately he succeeded Perregaux
as the head of the concern, and thereafter, until his
indiscreet blending of politics with finance brought
about a result almost inevitable in France in those
days of intrigue and faction, he was one of the
greatest powers in the country. As governor of
the Bank of France he financed Louis XVIII in
1814, while it was in Laffitte's bank that Napoleon,
on the eve of sailing for St. Helena, deposited five
million francs in gold. Perhaps the best deed of
Laffitte's career was to supply from his own pocket
two million francs for the arrears of pay of the
Imperial troops after Waterloo.

Jacques Laffitte became a deputy in 1816. In
1830 he was active in the Revolution to remove
Charles X, the Bourbon, and it was he who, as
President of the Chamber of Deputies, offered the
crown to Louis Philippe, the Orleanist. A year
later, however, after every kind of disaffection in the
country, Louis Philippe made Laffitte's degrada-
tion a sop to the mob, and the banker retired into
private life a ruined man, begging pardon of God
for having assisted an ungrateful master to the

throne.   I wish I could associate his name also with almost the best claret that the Medoc produces, but the word Lafite of Chateau Lafite has but one 'f' and one 't', and can be traced back to the thirteenth century. No one, however, seems to know its origin.

It would round off your reflections on the rise and fall of the financier and wire-puller if after leaving Breteuil-sur-Iton you passed on to Dreux, taking Verneuil, with its glorious church tower, on the way; for at Dreux, high on a hill, rises the stately mausoleum of the Orleans family—the Chapelle Royale St. Louis which the Dowager Duchess of Orleans began in 1816 and her son Louis Philippe completed, and in which he and his queen Amelia are, I suppose, the most notable figures.   Compared with the elaborate, dazzling, full-length, realistic statue of the dapper, fobbed and whiskered King beside his Queen, in the upper crypt, with the life of the Orleanist St. Louis in coloured glass all around, the weather-stained bust of Laffitte in the open air at Breteuil is mediocre indeed; but had Laffitte lived he would have seen Time's revenges at work, for in 1848 another Revolution turned Louis Philippe from the throne, forcing him to escape with his Queen to England, travelling as Mr. and Mrs. Smith, and to spend the embittered evening of life in exile at Claremont, near Esher, where he died in 1850.   His Queen survived till

1866, dying at Weybridge, but both were re-united in this French chapel.

The austerity of the architecture, hardly softened by the coloured glass, much of which reproduces designs from the supreme but frigid hand of Ingres; the whiteness of the marble effigies, most of them recumbent; the tragedy of the Orleanist cause—all contribute to make this splendid temple of death a more than usually gloomy place. But I think the most depressing influence emanates from the tomb of the Duchesse d'Alençon, that gracious, philanthropical lady who was burned to death in the Paris bazaar and who is represented here in her death agony. Sculptors should not be allowed to do things like that. As a contrast we have the stately dignity of the Duc d'Aumale, with his rapier in his hand: that generous and enlightened nobleman who made Chantilly into a treasure-house and left it to the Academicians of France as a national possession, together with a row of houses in the park for any of the Forty who feel less immortal than usual to recuperate in and recover their confidence.

A GREEDY MAP

THERE is spread out before me on my table,
to the obliteration of all practical things,
such as matches, books of reference,
matches, stamps, date calendar, matches, ink, clips,
matches, a very formidable map. Its title is *Carte
Gastronomique de la France*, the delineator is A.
Bourguignon, ex-chef de cuisine, and it is under
the patronage of that illustrious personage M. Curnonsky, 'Prince des Gastronomes'. M. Curnonsky,
by the way, not only is the Prince of Gastronomes
but is President of the Academy of Gastronomes
(where, I suppose, as Wordsworth would say, you
see Forty eating like one), and as such lends authority
to a little pocket-book first published in 1930,
entitled *Où déjeunons-nous?* (a very proper question),
giving no fewer than four thousand addresses all
over France. He has also, in collaboration with
M. Bienstock, formed two collections of the
wittiest and raciest French anecdotes. A man to
know.

The greedy map, which was given to me by an
English lady whose banquets are renowned for their

excellence and abundance, is simple in scheme: to record against every town or province its special delicacy, from Calais in the North ('biscuits, conserves de poisson, pâtes alimentaires'), reckoning fish as nothing, to Banyuls in the South ('langouste en civet, nougats'); from Crozon in the West ('homards de cameret') to Strasburg in the East, with a list too long to quote, headed by la choucroute and not disregarding the liver of our sister the goose.

Between these extremes the fair land of France flaunts everything that the hungry can deal with or the gluttonous desire: so much, indeed, that after a few minutes poring over it my thoughts have been turning longingly towards dry bread, locusts and wild honey, and the oatmeal on which the early Edinburgh Reviewers cultivated literature, to say nothing of the water of the spring. I would not swear that, among this rich profusion, I was not tempted now and again by the vision even of a bowl of skilly.

It is amusing to think of the different ways in which a place can be looked at. Ruskin, for example, thought of Amiens as a centre of sublime and inspired architecture, and wrote *The Bible of Amiens* in its praise; to M. Bourguignon Amiens is noteworthy for les macarons and les pâtes de canard. To me the little town of Moret-sur-Loing is sacred as the home of Alfred Sisley; but M. Bourguignon, seeing the name, has sticky lips as he thinks of the sucre d'orge made there by the religieuses. Where Walter Pater, as I have been saying in this book, found in Auxerre the materials for the construction of a legendary figure, a pagan in a Christian environment, M. Bourguignon finds snails. When we reach that inland city which provided Lord Lytton, the dramatist, with a heroine, there is an array of comestibles, triumphant in large type, which by their luxuriousness causes the spirits of the dyspeptically disposed once again to sink.

Marvellous fellows, the French! How can the people of Lyon, one wonders, ever have any appetite left? But they and M. Bourguignon and, for all I know, the great Curnonsky, Prince of Gastronomes, are undefeatable. Nor to them has Lyon anything to do with silk; Lyon is the home of les morilles à la crême, of le poulet célestine, of les quenelles de brochet, of le gras-double lyonnaise, of les pommes de terre aux oignons, and a dozen savoury things beside. Does nothing cloy? Nothing. Arles, where Roman remains crumble beneath tropical sun, is, we find, honoured for its sausages, and Orleans is famed less for the Maid than for its vinegar, its pâtes de coings and its terrines de volaille. What a map for the gourmand aviator! From the security of the zenith he could descend wherever his palate decreed.

It would never, I am sure, occur to any English cook to make a similar chart of her own country; but it could, of course, be done. Not with such results as this French one, of course, nor with such evenly distributed productiveness; and, of course, there would be none of the vintages which lend so much colour to M. Bourguignon's projection. A few districts, such as Burton and Romford and London, might be tinted brown for beer, and Devonshire and Herefordshire green for cider: that is the most we could do. Cheese and hams would offer opportunities. Kent would be associated with hops and cherries; Worcestershire with plums and asparagus; Bath and Chelsea with buns; Everton with toffee; Eccles with cakes; Warsash with crabs and lobsters; Wales with rarebits; Whitstable, Colchester, and the Helston river with oysters; Bath with Olivers; Tunbridge Wells with those delicious wafers called Romarys; Yarmouth with bloaters; Harrogate with toffee; Doncaster with butter-scotch; the two burys—Ban and Shrews —with cakes; Devonshire with junket and cream; Dover with soles; Pontefract with licorice; and the South Downs with mutton.

Enough, however, of food. The kind of map that I should like to see, or even to help to construct, would mark the towns and villages of England where the best old curiosity shops and old book shops are to be found. Just as the A.A. and R.A.C. handbooks give garages and motor repairers, so would we give dealers in antiquities. The compilation would need constant care, for whereas in the alimentary products of France there is stability, the old curiosity shops and old book shops disappear or change hands, and in changing hands too often lose merit. Marseille (you must excuse this return to the carte gastronomique, but I need an illustration), Marseille will continue to produce la bouillabaisse, Bar-le-Duc its confitures des groseilles, and Pont l'Evêque its fromage, for ever, but Beauchamp Place, for all the pine-wood pieces, the green glass, the samplers and the objets d'art that adorn it at the moment, may one day be nothing but a nest of milliners. That old curiosity shop at Winchester which once was so well-stored, is it there to-day? That charming old lady in the little corner house in Bath, with odd jewellery, has she been superseded? Alas, only too probably, for it is the rule of life. Change! Change! Everywhere, that is, except as regards the alimentary products of France. Isigny, for instance—but enough!

MONET AT GIVERNY

WHEN an eminent authentic man reaches a great age, with a distinguished career behind him, and his sympathy still quick for the others, and his faculties about him, enjoying the evening of life—how excellent a thing that a friend with tablets should draw him out in conversation and make a record of the result! We don't want to bother him to sit down and write: he has earned that immunity, and, moreover, few octogenarians, even though good talkers, can be trusted to be interesting with a pen; but what a pity that so many memories and so much ripeness should be lost! That is why I like the sumptuous book entitled *A Giverny chez Claude Monet*, containing notes of the things the old landscape painter was saying, in his last days, to M. Marc Elder.

The book is of peculiar interest to me because I myself was at Giverny in the autumn of 1924, and before me stands a signed photograph of the master in his garden—a riot of Michaelmas daisies, asters in clumps, and nasturtiums writhing over the paths like snakes. The nasturtiums struck a

VACHES À L'ABREUVOIR

TROYON

From the picture in the Louvre

more violent chord than we are accustomed to in this artist's work; but the Michaelmas daisies held the mauve and violet that he has loved so well.

The painter told me that these nasturtiums were encouraged to encroach and run wild largely because his friend Clemenceau insisted upon it. Since then the Tiger wrote a book in praise of Monet; and now they are both no more. Friendships between statesmen and painters are not frequent, or at any rate they seldom lead to books. So far as I know, Palmerston wrote nothing about Turner, nor have we any news, in the Literary Gossip columns, that our own Prime Minister is preparing a work on Sir George Clausen, though he might do worse.

I found Monet still hale, although born as long ago as 1840, painting a little every day, staining his fingers with innumerable cigarettes of black tobacco, firing off sententiæ, and in the evenings playing backgammon on a lordly table. A burly man, very carefully and individually dressed, with a big white beard. I wish I could describe the sensitive eyes that for so long had been searching for beauty beneath the changing skies and finding it and capturing it for others to rejoice in, too; but his dark spectacles hid them.

Monet's eyes—what marvellous organs! With

the exception of Turner, I suppose that no other painter has been so possessed by the desire to conquer the mysteries of light; and not even Turner, so far as I know, gave the time that this patient Frenchman would spend on one object during different hours and different seasons—whether it was the façade of Rouen Cathedral, a row of poplars, or a haystack in the snow. For many persons Monet may be said to have discovered, or indeed invented, the poplar. At any rate, until he came to see a row of those temperamental trees with his analytic vision, most of us had given no thought to their place in the chromatic scale. Green we should have called them, with a tendency to silver in the wind. But Claude Monet's eyes found in them hints of every delicate hue. One of his stories to M. Elder tells how he was at work on a poplar series, painting the same trees, according to his wont, in shine and shade, at dawn, at noon, and at dusk, when word came that the land on which they grew was to be sold and the timber felled. To a conscientious artist this was an intolerable situation; so what did he, but buy the property himself, holding it until his task was finished?

In Clemenceau's book on Monet is a curious passage, following upon his remark that they— the two friends—saw things differently: he, the practical man, seeing them as they superficially

are; the other, the artist, analytically and synthetic-
ally, looking beneath the surface to divide the object
into particles of light. The late John S. Sargent,
with his accustomed directness, frankly called it
astigmatism. In a letter to the Duke of Alba,
printed in Mr. Charteris's admirable memoir, Sargent
says roundly, 'The colouring of Claude Monet is
an absolutely genuine document, perhaps the only
genuine one, of the optical phenomena of astigmatism.'

'You cannot understand', Monet replied to M.
Clemenceau, 'how true is all that you say. It is
the joy and the torment of my life. So much
so that one day, finding myself at the bedside of
one who had been and would always be very dear
to me, I caught myself, my eyes fixed on the tragic
brow, in the act of mechanically looking for the
tones that death had just engraved on the still face.
Tones of blue, of yellow, of grey—how many?
That is where I had got to. It is only natural
to wish to reproduce the last picture of one who
is going to leave us for ever. But even before
the thought came to fix for ever the features I was
so fond of, I was automatically moved by the colours,
in the unconscious manner which was a part of
my everyday life, and the reflexes interested me in
spite of myself. But enough of the beast who
turns the mill-stone. Pity me, my friend.'

It was M. Clemenceau who, after years of official neglect had, if not embittered, at any rate not gladdened, the artist's evening, made it easy for the series of tone-dreams called the 'Nymphéas', or water-lilies, to be housed proudly in the Orangery of the Tuileries as a national possession; and it was upon this last work that Monet was engaged when I went to see him. First he showed us the lake at the foot of his garden, and then he showed us his studio round which the panels were ranged. Although the painter had recently had an operation for cataract, and could see, but dimly, with but one eye, he persisted in undertaking the terrific task of translating the amethystine depths of his water-garden into pigment. I expressed admiration of the achievement, but the painter shook his head. 'When I look at the work of others,' he said, 'I see only its merits; when I look at my own, I see only its faults.'

Among the many artists whom Monet recalled with affection or admiration, in his talks with M. Elder, perhaps the most interesting are Manet, Cézanne, and Jongkind. Since most new-comers to French painting begin with a little perplexity over the likeness of the two names Manet and Monet, it is comforting to read that the first words that Monet ever heard Manet utter bore upon this confusion. It was at the Salon of 1865, where the youthful Monet had two pictures. 'It is disgusting', cried Manet (who was then thirty-three) to a neighbouring group of artists, 'the way I am being congratulated on two pictures by a fellow named Monet. If the boy has any success,' he added, 'it will be because his name can be taken for mine.' Later the two men became fast friends. 'The art of Manet', says Monet, 'was a revelation to me. Afterwards I evolved.'

Cézanne he called 'a being impossible to define', whom none of his biographical critics have rightly described. An impish, ironical turn forced him often to appear below his best, while he deliberately exaggerated his provincialism. On meeting Manet, who was a dandy, at a café, Cézanne excused himself from shaking hands by saying that he hadn't washed his for eight days. Monet said he never knew when Cézanne was being serious. When asked once to Giverny, Cézanne declined the invitation but added, 'The friendship of a great man is a blessing of the gods.' To this Monet appended the phrase, 'Drôle de corps!' but Cézanne may have meant no harm. 'The Flaubert of painting,' Monet called him, adding, 'When he is good, he is excellent, and even his errors are lessons. . . . He thought only of painting, loved nothing else. And he never compromised.' Renoir, he says, was equally a devotee. Too many of the artists of our day, Monet thought, lack such concentration. He found a certain idleness, a certain tendency to least resistance. 'They content themselves with the possession of a talent and with honourable intentions.'

Monet admired Corot fully, but was sad that he never appreciated 'our movement'—that is to say, Impressionism. Daumier was another god, and it was a great grief to him that on the occasion when they met and a picture of Monet's was being examined Daumier said nothing. Diaz, on the contrary, was enthusiastic. 'Very kind of him,' said Monet, 'but Diaz wasn't Daumier.' That wild creature, Jongkind, a glorious pleinairiste, was an early friend of Monet's at Havre, when Boudin was his companion. Jongkind, said Monet, was a child, sensitive and delicious, but an enfant terrible. There is a good story of his impact on Monet's parents, who, wishing to see the painter who had encouraged their son, asked him to dinner. With him came a lady, who, in course of time, was addressed as Madame Jongkind. At this Jongkind began to roar with laughter. 'She's not Madame Jongkind,' he explained, to the horror of his exceedingly comme-il-faut host and hostess, 'she's not my wife—she's an angel.' He then related how this lady, Madame Tesser, had come to his rescue when he was a drunkard and an outcast, and had given him back his confidence and self-respect.

So much for Monet among the artists. Less thrilling, although not without interest, is the revelation that he was devoted to rhubarb tart.

NAPOLEON'S END

NAPOLEONIC relics are very widely distributed. I have seen them at Malmaison, at the Invalides, at the Carnavalet, at Fontainebleau, at Compiègne, at Madame Tussaud's, at the United Service Museum in Whitehall; and more recently at the Bodleian, where there is a collection of Napoleoniana, bequeathed by Lord Curzon of Kedleston, which all admirers of the amazing meteor should study. It is a melancholy assemblage, for all the emphasis is laid upon St. Helena. There is some furniture, but it is merely of the epoch, without personal association; and there is the remarkable series of grangerized Napoleonic books to which Mr. A. M. Broadley dedicated his leisure; but these are not accessible to the casual visitor. The rest of the collection consists of prints, lithographs, and drawings bearing upon the period of exile.

Here you will find the Emperor in his great planter's hat loitering in the garden; the Emperor looking out over the waste of waves towards France; several versions of the Emperor on his deathbed, one by Captain Marryat, the novelist; a picture of the actual death-chamber on May 5, 1821, very dramatic in treatment, by Steuben, with the stricken attendants all about; and a frame of relics: a wisp of Napoleon's hair; his signature six months before death, very shaky; a pencilled note signed 'J. W.' describing Napoleon's countenance immediately after death and running thus: 'The face had a re-markably placid expression, and indicated mildness and sweetness of disposition. Those who gazed on the features, as they lay in the still repose of death, could not help exclaiming, "How beautiful!" The head was so large as to be disproportioned to the rest of the body.'

Afterwards hunting about for some Napoleonic literature, I came upon an English translation, published many years ago, of a biography by Laurent de l'Ardèche, a popular work with five hundred designs by Horace Vernet, one of the first of them displaying a fat naked baby, with the head already far too big, crawling upon what one would take to be a rug, but which the text tells us was the piece of tapestry embroidered with bellicose identical episodes from the 'Iliad' on which Signora Bonaparte, taken unawares, suddenly lay in, and which the biographer, a very simple gentle-man, believes to have exercised an influence upon the infant's career. Maternity homes, please note.

M. de l'Ardèche, who at Longwood devotedly follows Las Cases, makes the last phase sufficiently miserable, humiliating, and tragic. To him, as to Lord Rosebery, Sir Hudson Lowe is unpardonable. Horace Vernet follows the artist of the well-known 'planter' sketch, to which I have referred, and gives us more than one variant. In one, Napoleon is seen talking to Toby, a negro who had been captured and sold by an English slaver, and was now employed as gardener at Briars, the house in which Napoleon resided until Longwood was ready for him. The Emperor, who wished to buy Toby's freedom, 'never spoke of his abduction but with the greatest indignation'. Toby led to a very interesting monologue. 'If', said Napoleon, 'this crime be the act of the English captain alone, he is doubtless one of the vilest of men; but if it be that of the whole of the crew, it may have been committed by men, perhaps, not so base as might be imagined; for vice is always individual, and scarcely ever collective. Joseph's brethren could not bring themselves to slay him; while Judas, a cool, hypocritical, calculating villain, betrayed his master.'

And again: 'When I acquired the supreme direction of affairs, it was wished that I might become a Washington. Words cost nothing; and no doubt those who were so ready to express the wish did so without any knowledge of times, place, persons, or things. Had I been in America I would willingly have been a Washington, and I should have had little merit in so being; for I do not see how I could reasonably have acted otherwise. But had Washington been in France, exposed to discord within and invasion from without, I would have defied him to have been what he was in America; at least, he would have been a fool to attempt it, and would only have prolonged the existence of evil. For my own part, I could only have been a *Crowned Washington*. It was only in a congress of kings, in the midst of kings, yielding or subdued, that I could become so. Then and there alone I could successfully display Washington's moderation, disinterestedness, and wisdom.' When at Briars, says M. de l'Ardèche, Napoleon played hide-and-seek with the children of the house. At Longwood he taught the girls to play billiards.

One coloured picture in the Curzon collection shows the body being taken to its resting-place, under the weeping willow, in May, 1821; another depicts the cortège descending the hill on October 15, 1840, bringing the remains down to the ship which was to carry them to France for reburial in the chapel of the Invalides, under the massive tomb that one sees there to-day. M. de l'Ardèche's book has an appendix describing the exhumation of

6

Napoleon's remains on October 15, 1840. According to an eyewitness, 'when the satin sheet was raised, an indescribable feeling of surprise and affection was exhibited by the spectators, most of whom burst into tears. The Emperor himself was before their eyes! The features of his face, though changed, were perfectly recognized—the hands perfectly beautiful—his well-known costume had suffered but little, and the colours were easily distinguished—the epaulettes, the decorations, and the hat, seemed to be entirely preserved from decay; the attitude itself was full of ease, and but for the fragments of the satin lining, which covered as with a fine gauze several parts of the uniform, it might have been believed that Napoleon was before them, extended on a bed of state.' The body was conveyed from Val de la Haye, on the right bank of the Seine near Rouen, to Courbevoie, a few miles from Paris, by barge. At Courbevoie it was transferred to a magnificent car and passed in procession to the Invalides, where it was deposited on December 15, 1840.

On leaving the Bodleian, I noticed on the way to the station several hoardings on which, among many posters, was one belonging to a firm of tailors depicting Napoleon's most familiar attire, disposed as though being worn, even with the right arm crossed, but containing nothing. This design was accompanied by the motto, 'Clothes make the man'. I thought this an odd statement to come upon so soon after the Bodleian exhibition; yet did not Chateaubriand say, after the fall, that the grey great-coat and the hat of Napoleon, if placed on a stick on the Brest shore, would make all Europe run to arms?

THE ARTIST OF THE INN

SHOULD any student of Napoleon's history wish to see the point where his body was trans-shipped, he will find an obelisk commemorating the event, the date on it being December 9, 1840. Val de la Haye, I should point out, is only a tiny village which, should one be arriving by road through La Grande Couronne on the other side of this strangely winding river, has to be reached by ferry. The last bridge over the Seine being at Rouen itself, all these lower sinuosities are crossed by bacs or served by passenger steamers, many of them probably paddle-boats still; for the inhabitants of this riparian district of Normandy are still simple and unsophisticated and without other ambition than to fill the stomach and not leave the stocking empty.

Hence the ferry boats are primitive affairs, still propelled slantwise against the tide by oars, or, if they are the larger ones, to carry vehicles, towed by a rowing boat, with no protection whatever against rain or wind, both of which too often select Normandy for their home; while the ferry-men are

LE MARAIS

DAUBIGNY

From the picture in the Louvre

primitive too, unhastening and taciturn, with chests and arms like giants'. On the day when I had made Val de la Haye my goal it was fortunately very hot, so that the wait at the ferry on the Grande Couronne side—while Charon first was summoned from his lunch by the bell, and then was deciding whether or not to obey it, and then, after calling his assistant from some other lunch table, was making the transit, with a narrow escape from a collier in mid-stream—was not in the least irksome. In fact, I think that, under agreeable conditions, waiting for the ferry is one of the pleasantest ways of passing time that can be devised.

Having scrutinized the monument, my next and imperative duty was to find an inn: a simple task, for there was but one, the Hostellerie du Méridian, a crazy old house at the water's edge, with a sundial on its façade, and, inside, the prettiest yellow panels and yellow ceilings and yellow crockery and yellow candle-shades and blue-and-white table-cloths and napkins. This Hostellerie I shall always remember, not only on account of a Normandy speciality, consisting of very thin rashers of bacon curled up within a casing of batter, which restored me to life again; but because it was there that I met M. Conrad.

On the walls of the old winding staircase, with its wide, shallow steps and terrific oak rampe, I had noticed some vigorous black-and-white drawings of historical scenes, some landscapes and pencil sketches very delicate in quality, and one or two harmless French naughtinesses, all signed Conrad, while there were also votive pictures to their ami Conrad from other artists. M. Conrad, I thought, stays here from time to time, and very wisely. But I was to find that his association with the inn was closer than that, for he was the landlord, and probably still is. I hope so. That he had made himself a real home I can testify, for he led me to the top floor of this amazing Louis XIII structure, in which, in a great attic, everything that an historical painter can require was to be found: an easel, hundreds of brushes and tubes, costumes, armour, a lay figure, books of reference, and, above all, myriad sketches of old courtyards, old houses, old churches, old châteaux, faithfully recorded, to be used as background in the artist's illustrations. A copy of Gautier's *Le Capitaine Fracasse*, with a spirited swashbuckling commentary, in the tradition of M. Mauriel Leloir, from M. Conrad's pencil, lay on the table. But this was not the extent of the gifts of this bewildering publican, for he had a forge at the foot of the garden in which he did smith work. His bed was of iron, his dressing-table was of iron, very beautifully convoluted, both wrought by his own hands.

This was in the days before I had been made welcome by Mr. John Fothergill, the animal painter, at the Spread Eagle at Thame, in our own country; and now that I have seen both I am persuaded that more artists should take to inn-keeping.   It is just the life for these unbustled, amiable creatures, who are superior to all the social caste nonsense.   Not having to worry with kitchen duties, for those can be delegated, they are thus left free to hang about with cigarettes and gossip, to assemble interesting pictures, and, when it is fine and customers are few, get on with their painting, and when customers are few and it is wet, to take stock of the cellar, or indite to their friends those illustrated letters which it is the glorious privilege of artists to send forth.   I can think, at the moment, of several R.A.'s and A.R.A.'s who would be all the better for keeping inns.

A PHILANTHROPIST

HE was that often-very-wise man, an old American traveller, and we shared a little table in a wagon-lit restaurant, where, even for so diffident a person as myself, it is almost impossible to withhold conversation. As for my companion, silence was to him unknown, and, naturally, since we were eating our way through the fair land of France, it was of France and the French that he talked: always a sound topic, in all nations provocative of candour.

'They're an odd bunch, the French,' he said, 'but I like them more than not. They have ways that irritate me, such as not being able to see without staring; and having only one idea at a time; and preferring leatherette to leather; and not letting partridges hang; and drinking their claret cold; and not heating the plates; and being so indifferent to the beauty of flowers; and in the pension hotels getting more and more fond of that infernal kill-joy, the paper napkin. But I like them. They're quick and happy and jocular; they don't mind how near the road they fix their picnics; they dress for them-

LE CHEMIN DE SÈVRES

COROT

From the picture in the Louvre

selves and not for others; and they don't allow
newspaper posters.

'And, take it all round, they run their country
well.   Well enough, at any rate, for the French.
It's a country fit for Frenchmen to live in, as your
Mr. Lloyd George might say.   When I first came
over many years ago I expected to find the United
States wherever I went, and I was very critical
when they were missing.   But I've long got over
such nonsense.   I now leave the United States
behind me at Cherbourg or Southampton or
wherever I get off and try to belong to the new
land.

'But although I've learned to like the French
and even to believe that, if I were given the chance
of a second time on earth and might choose my
nationality, I would elect to be a Frenchman, there
are two places where I can't follow them.   First, into
their post offices.   When it comes to post offices
I withdraw everything good I've said about France.
They are so incredibly bad that one is amazed that
the revolutionary spirit, which used to be so active,
never awakes to burn them.   I myself never enter
one to-day: I pay others to do so; but if I had again
the hours I have spent there, trying to get a letter
from the Poste Restante, trying to get a stamp,
trying to send a telegram, my death would be
postponed for years and years.   If it had been in

my nature to shove I might die a little earlier, for some of the lost time was captured by other customers forcing their way out of their places into mine. But I can't shove.

'And when you've got the telegram across and the assistant has finished writing a book about it and given you the change, what confidence have you that it will ever be sent? None. And what confidence have you that your letters will be delivered? None. Unless they're registered, when the postman is as punctual as Fate and as irresistible, breaking even into your bedroom.

'Pass over the distressing themes of the ink, the pens, the blotting-paper, and come to the second place where the French fail me—in their drugstores, or, as you would say, their chemists' shops. Not that these are scandalous like the post offices, but they're without authority. They don't look right. You can't believe the clerk knows, and when it's a matter of physic of course he ought to know. That's his sole reason for existence. And it may be a question of life or death.

'For the French they're good enough. The French don't approach physic as they approach food; they're casual about it, and in point of fact are rarely ill; but it matters to us, because when we're ill we're really ill and we know what we want. But suppose we can't speak enough French, what

check have we on these dope-merchants? None.
Do you know that I've motored thousands of miles
in France and I've been in hundreds of drug-stores
—for I'm a bit of a sufferer, as a man is apt to be
when he's past three-score-and-ten—and I've never
found an English-French dictionary in one of them.
Not one! So where are you when you know what
you need but can't ask for it?

'Of course there ought to be an Esperanto for
medicaments. There would be in a sensible world.
But of course there isn't, and at this very moment
in a drug-store in that town over there among the
trees there may be an American or an Englishman
with dyspepsia crying for peppermint and getting
prussic acid. It's a solemn thought.'

For a second—a second only—he paused. And
then he resumed. 'So what do you think I'm going
to do when I get home?' he asked. 'Mr. Rocke-
feller, who's a fine old fellow even if he can't grow
any hair, gives his money to schools, while the late
Andrew Carnegie endowed libraries, and to a
certain extent I am copying them. Directly I get
back I'm going to see my lawyer and arrange for
a fund to supply every French drug-store with a
dictionary—yes, and a chain to hold it, like the
Bible in your old churches—so that there won't be
so many mistakes as there are to-day, and your
countrymen and mine—the salt of the earth—will

have a chance. Hey? What do you know about that?'

I said—and it was the first remark I had the chance of making—that I thought it was sound and that he was in the direct line of common sense from that great laughing philosopher and American ambassador to France, Benjamin Franklin. Nothing could have given him more pleasure.

HOME AGAIN

3.40—We reach Le Bourget aerodrome. There are ten of us. I don't like the look of the sky. There is a terribly disconcerting noise coming from the aeroplanes on the ground. Trying the engines, it is called, but it tries me too. I wonder why I decided to fly?

3.45—We are being weighed. The official puts our names on a paper. The weighing-machine moves from side to side in such a manner as to suggest that we are not sober; but I am. I rather wish I wasn't. Dutch courage! The luggage is being weighed too. Those of us who don't object to publicity are writing their names, addresses and professions in a book; but there is no compulsion. Whether we like it or not, our bags, even the little ones, are being covered with labels, pasted on and very difficult to get off. Our passports have been taken away by a French official.

3.50.—We are now in the departure-room, waiting for our passports back. An official has just asked me if I want to insure my life. For a thousand pounds. It seems to me an inadequate sum. Surely my life is worth more than that; but I shouldn't get it, anyway. I wish, however, that he hadn't asked me. It has made me nervous. Very dangerous things, aeroplanes; heavier than air and therefore against Nature. The railway is best, but I can't change now; too late; besides, that also would require courage.

3.52.—Another official has just asked me if I am taking more than ten thousand francs out of the country. I am not. I wish I had the chance.

3.55.—We are still awaiting our passports.

4.0.—Time to go, but no passports yet. I can't forget about that fellow suggesting that I should insure my life. At one moment I think it ominous; at another I think it promises well, because no company wants a man to be killed after only one premium.

4.5.—An official says that there is delay with baggage. What fun if it refused to start and we couldn't go at all! Another nice dinner in Paris!

4.8.—No luck! Here are the passports and we are free to get into the aeroplane.

4.10.—In. It is long and narrow, with little wicker arm-chairs tilted back and fixed to the floor, and a tin pan under each. The tin pan is in case of sickness.

4.13.—The door has been bolted. All hope abandon. Perhaps I ought to have taken out that policy. If I've got to die, why not sting a company and enrich a friend?

4.14.—The propellers are let loose. The noise is deafening, and we stuff cotton-wool, provided for the purpose, into our ears.

4.15.—We move forward.

4.16.—We are rushing over the ground. It is very bumpy, but after all it is the earth. Dear earth!

4.17.—We are in the air. It is a strange sensation. Do I like it? No. But I can't get out. Horrible air!

4.17.—We are rising higher and higher. The hangars below us are diminishing and receding. I wish I was on my flat feet on the good solid ground. How jolly even to be sloshing through mud!

4.20.—We are going at the rate of eighty miles an hour. Farewell beautiful, friendly Paris; farewell, welcoming, smiling maîtres d'hôtel; farewell, kind, solicitous waiters!

4.23.—We are over a tremendous forest with a château in it. I unfold the map. I'll die busy, anyway.

4.24.—We are over a river. It is the Wahz. The French spell it Oise, but Wahz is what they mean. There is a manufacturing town below us, half called Beaumont and half Persan.

4.25.—Now the square fields and white roads and

great woods. France is a gigantic country, with almost no towns in it at all and not very noticeable villages.

4.29.—We are going over one of the villages. It is very long and has two factory chimneys, one church and one big house not quite a château.

4.30.—Now the fields again and some more vast woods.

4.31.—We are in a thunderstorm and rocking violently, but no one seems to mind. In front of me two Americans are laffing.

4.32.—The storm is behind us and we are steady again.

4.35.—We are over a town with streets and squares and factories, a very big cemetery and a mammoth church. Also a smaller church, both without spires. It is Beauvais, and at the factories they make tapestry. I know the mammoth church or cathedral. It has the highest walls I ever saw and beautiful white windows with old glass in the middle or at the top only. There is a blue astronomical clock there with silver chimes, very sweet, and the town has a local Joan of Arc all its own named Jeannette Hachette, who did something so heroic and necessary that she has a statue in the Grande Place. Beauvais has some wonderful old houses, but would have none had the German Air Force been more successful with their bombs. I do not see all this from my seat; I knew it before.   The Americans are trying to photograph it.   Their open window makes an insupportable draught.

4.40.—We are all among the parallelograms again; some light-green, some dark, some yellow, some brown, according to the crops.   The sun is out and the shadow of the aeroplane sweeps over the ground after us.   A railway line winds below us. Here is another château, bleak and lonely, as they all are, without any lawns or flowers or tennis-courts as in England.   Almost no one is seen in the fields, but there are cattle and sheep.   No cars are to be seen on the white roads, some winding, but most straight.

4.42.—Our shadow has just rushed through a flock of geese.   Now it has dashed across a plough-man and his horses, one white.   I wonder what he says to his team.   What is the French for 'Gee-up' and 'Whoa'?

4.50.—The first water since the Wahz, and this only a stream.   We are going straight into another black storm.   I have now forgotten all about dying.   I think these planes must be fairly stable, accidents are so rare.   Flying really is the only civilized way of getting about.

4.51.—Here is a valley full of villages with a railway running down it.   Poor old obsolete rail-way!   In a field is a strange red obelisk.

7

4.53.—The rain is terrific and we are now like *Peter Schlemihl*.

4.55.—Here is the sun again.   And here are two windmills.   How odd to have no hedges!   Not only does this necessitate girls and women to act as cowherds and shepherds, but how can a French farmer tell where his land stops?   We have a shadow again.   If we are going at the rate of ninety miles an hour, so is the shadow.

5.0.—After the storms, the wet tarmac roads are like canals between the high poplars, which down there look tall, but to us are mere shrubs.   Here is another winding stream.

5.1.—Another valley with villages and a railway. In the distance, in the east, are lakes and marshes— I guess they are those the train passes between Boulogne and Paris.   The train—how futile!

5.7.—We are now over a bigger river and the railway with marshes beside it.   The plane is very steady.   I'm glad I didn't pay that premium.

5.9.—We have just passed over Abbeville and its flying ground.   In the west the sun is shining on estuary inlets and the sea glittering beyond.   It is getting rougher, but none of us has heeded the call of the tin.

5.15.—The widest forest of all is now below us —miles and miles of it.   It is an hour since we started.

LES PEUPLIERS

MONET

From the picture in the Tate Gallery

5.17.—The end of the forest and some more marshes.

5.25.—Another estuary on the left and the sea-front of a watering-place, with fishing-boats dotting the silver.

5.29.—We are crossing the river that runs out at Le Touquet. Below is Etaples.

5.30.—Here are the sand-dunes, and sheep cropping the pré-salé grass. If I were back in Paris I would order a little saddle. Never mind, it will be easy to go over again next week. Flying is so simple.

5.35.—We are now over the woods and sand-dunes behind Hardelot. A very black Channel awaits us. Boulogne is ahead on the right.

5.37.—We are over the sea, a little to the left of Boulogne. Farewell to France.

5.38.—The harbour is below with two dredgers in it. Very green and calm. A Channel steamer is on its way to Folkestone. That's a dull way to travel. Over there on the right are the sands of Wimereux. It is getting thick and foggy. I take refuge in a detective story.

6.0.—Folkestone is emerging from the mist and we are making straight for it.

6.2.—We are over Hythe, very wet from recent rain, and another storm coming directly. It is

difficult to distinguish the roads from the canal.
There is a car here and there.   Men at work, men
who speak English.

6.3.—Now the fields begin, all pasture and all the
same green, and no longer parallelograms and no
longer without hedges.   Now and then there is a
crop, but very seldom, for the sheep rule here.
They move like maggots.   A stranger looking down
from this height would be puzzled to explain them,
especially as some have recently been shorn and some
haven't.   Everything is green but an occasional
elder-bush in bloom.

6.10.—The hop gardens have begun and the
gentlemen's places—all so much more comfortable-
looking than the French châteaux, and all with
flower-gardens and kitchen-gardens and lawn-tennis
courts and often a lake.   The villages don't seem
to be so numerous as in France, but there are more
houses in between: farms with outbuildings and
hop-oasts, ponds and orchards, cottages and week-
end retreats.   England seems to be more lived-in
than France.

6.20.—We are over a straggling village on the
main line, but I can't identify it.   My map is a
French one.   There is a white windmill.   Now
comes another storm, making the aeroplane very
cold and obliterating the landscape.

6.24.—Finer.   Just on the right is a very large

park with a white mansion, glass-houses and all the rest of it.

6.29.—We have just crossed a river; I know it to be the Medway.

6.30.—There is a wonderful estate below us, with a mansion with domes, two dependencies, a great lake and formal gardens. I make a note to get a map of Kent and locate it.

6.31.—We are now over high common and woodland, sandy and wild. The brake fern is very green. What a lovely country England is! You should see it from the air. Everyone ought to fly to see England from the air.

6.35.—More high woods below and more big houses, chiefly red-brick. One of them has a green hard-court.

6.37.—We are over a sewage farm near a town.

6.40.—We are over a mansion with towers and a private cricket-ground. How unlike France! Another aeroplane is passing us, going east. Below they rake sodden hay.

6.42.—We are over a golf-links.

6.44.—We are over another golf-links. Here is Croydon.

6.45.—We begin to descend. All the houses are leaning over.

6.45½.—The engines have been shut off and a dense stunning peace has fallen. We fling away our cotton-wool and again converse. Total strangers talk familiarly, just because we are coming down from the sky. The aerodrome attendants are scuttling about.

6.46.—Solid earth.

6.48.—I get out and find myself very stiff. An official hands me a list of contraband articles. I light a cigarette.

6.50.—I approach the pilot and thank him for our safe passage. He says, 'Not at all'.

7.5.—I sink back in the motor-bus for London. Not a bad way of moving about the world, motoring.

NOTE

With the exception of two, all the foregoing essays appeared in the *Sunday Times*, and have been re-shaped for book form. My thanks are due to the proprietors for permission to reprint them. I also thank the proprietors of *Punch* for permission to reprint 'A Philanthropist'. The account of the air journey from Le Touquet to Croydon first appeared in *The Wag-Tale*, the magazine of the Westminster Hospital.

E. V. L.

Printed in Great Britain by
Butler & Tanner Ltd.,
Frome and London